Easy Steps To Lower Cholesterol

Easy Steps To Lower Cholesterol

The Portfolio Diet Action Plan

Veronica Rouse, MAN, RD, CDE

Created, reviewed and edited by: Veronica Rouse, MAN, RD, CDE

Photos by: © Kath Twigg at Kath Films

Cover design: Michael Lobsinger

Recipes & recipe photos by: Veronica Rouse, MAN, RD, CDE and nutrition students; Diksha Bansal, Shirley Le, Amanda Gracia, Francesca Badinotti, Marissa Frodsham, Aliza Hunt, Safura Husainy, Ndeye Fary Diop, Wesley Mai, Isabelle Mah, Sara Osia & Abina Chandrakumar.

ISBN: 9798322696551

Imprint: Independently published

First edition 2024 www.theheartdietitian.com

To all my clients, who have been my greatest teachers,

This book is dedicated to you. Your stories of challenge and victory shaped this book's approach, aiming to offer simple and accessible ways to integrate the principles of the Portfolio Diet into daily eating habits. Through thoughtful recipe modifications, small tweaks, and micro changes, I've strived to create a guide that leads to lasting health improvements.

I am deeply grateful for your trust and the invaluable lessons you've shared.

Contents

Smoothies

Breakfast

Lunch

Dinner

Snacks

Others

The Portfolio Diet

The Portfolio Diet - A Positive Message

The prevalence of heart disease is on the rise with an increasing focus on diets such as the Mediterranean diet, the DASH diet, and the vegetarian diet. However, not enough people have heard of the Portfolio Diet.

Dr. David Jenkins, a professor in the Departments of Medicine and Nutritional Sciences of the University of Toronto developed The Portfolio Diet with the aim of lowering one's cholesterol level and reducing the risk of coronary heart disease (1).

Concentrating on incorporating foods into our diet that are beneficial for heart health can enhance the strength of our heart. Previously, nutritional advice primarily centered on identifying which foods to reduce or eliminate to safeguard heart health. Recent studies, such as The Portfolio Diet, shift the focus towards identifying which foods we should consume daily to minimize the risk of heart disease. This diet doesn't eliminate any foods from your diet or specify which ingredients to limit.

So instead of focusing on foods to "avoid", we want to change the message to what foods can I "add" or "include." This is a more positive way of looking at health and an easier way to change eating patterns for the better.

This book will explore the mechanism of the Portfolio Diet and how you can easily incorporate it into your eating habits.

What Is The Portfolio Eating Pattern?

This way of eating is not just about losing weight; it's about improving overall health, particularly heart health. It's called the "Portfolio" Diet because, like a financial portfolio, it involves a diverse range of assets - in this case, food types - each contributing to the goal of improved health.

At its core, the Portfolio Diet focuses on incorporating a variety of cholesterol-lowering foods into your daily meals. These include soluble viscous fibers found in oats, barley, psyllium, eggplant, and okra; nuts like almonds and walnuts; soy proteins found in tofu and soy milk; and plant sterol-enriched products. What makes this diet stand out is its emphasis on adding these foods to your diet, rather than focusing on cutting out unhealthy ones.

The combination of eating these food groups every day maximizes the cholesterol-lowering benefits.

What Are The Benefits?

I'm sure you are wondering how much cholesterol-lowering does The Portfolio Diet actually offer?

The diet specifically lowers low-density lipoprotein (LDL) cholesterol which is often referred to as the "bad" cholesterol. LDL-cholesterol can build up in your arteries. If the build-up of cholesterol is in arteries carrying blood to and from the heart, the risk of a heart attack increases.

A one-year study by Dr. Jenkins monitored participants who followed the portfolio eating pattern under real-world conditions. Over 30% of participants who stuck to the diet saw over 20% decrease in LDL-cholesterol concentrations (2).

The diet has also been proven to lower other markers of cardiovascular disease risk, such as total cholesterol, blood pressure, triglycerides, and C-reactive protein (3).

Dr. Jenkins also conducted a study that directly compared the efficacy of The Portfolio Diet to a statin, a medication that lowers LDL cholesterol. Both significantly lower LDL-cholesterol levels as the statin medication decreased the LDL-cholesterol concentration by around 33% and the diet decreased LDL-cholesterol concentrations by around 30% after 4 weeks (4).

Thus, nutritional changes are considered a valuable form of cholesterol management.

Core Principals

The Portfolio Diet is grounded in a few fundamental principles:

- **Plant-Based Diversity**: Emphasizing a wide variety of plant-based foods.
- **Nutrient Density**: Focusing on foods rich in nutrients relative to their calorie content.
- **Heart Health**: Specifically designed to lower cholesterol and promote cardiovascular health.
- **Longevity:** Promoting dietary choices that support your health and well-being over the long term.

Key Components

Each component of the Portfolio Diet has been chosen for its specific health benefits, particularly its ability to lower cholesterol levels. Let's explore the benefits of each food component of The Portfolio Diet. The following recommended daily intakes are based on a standard 2,000-calorie diet.

1. Soluble Viscous Fiber

Soluble, or viscous fiber, thickens in the presence of water within our intestine which prevents cholesterol from entering the bloodstream. The gut bacteria also feed on the fiber to produce short-chain fatty acids that can lower the rate of cholesterol production in the liver (5).

Soluble fiber can be found in fruits, vegetables, legumes, and whole grains like oat bran. Consuming these foods should meet the recommended intake of 10-25 grams of viscous fiber (6).

Unfortunately, most people do not eat enough of these foods. However, there are simple solutions to increase your soluble fiber intakes such as adding more vegetables to your meals, snacking on fruits and vegetables, and opting for whole-grain cereals and baked goods.

When increasing your fiber intake, make sure you are also drinking enough water to prevent any digestive discomfort.

How does it work? Soluble fiber reduces cholesterol absorption in the intestines. It binds with cholesterol and bile acids (which are made partly from cholesterol) in the digestive system, forming a gel-like substance. Once bound, the cholesterol is entangled in this gel and not readily absorbed by the body. Instead, it's excreted as part of the body's waste. This process not only removes cholesterol directly but also prompts the liver to use up more cholesterol to replace bile acids, thus lowering the overall cholesterol level in the blood.

Impact on Cholesterol: Regular intake of soluble fiber can significantly lower total and LDL cholesterol levels.

Food Sources: Oats, barley, psyllium husk, avocado, legumes (like beans and lentils), fruits (like apples, oranges, and pears), and vegetables (like carrots and Brussels sprouts).

Benefits: Besides lowering cholesterol, soluble fiber aids in digestion, helps regulate blood sugar levels, and contributes to a feeling of fullness, aiding in weight management.

Nutrient Profile: These foods are a source of vitamins and minerals.

Daily Intake Goal: Aim for at least 10-25 grams of soluble fiber per day. This can be achieved through a combination of whole foods and fiber supplements if necessary.

2. Nuts

Nuts are a good source of fats, particularly healthy fats such as unsaturated and polyunsaturated fatty acids. Most people tend to shy away from fats because of common misconceptions about the health benefits and their high calories.

However, not only do the calories in nuts keep you full longer, but they may benefit your weight too. A review study found that eating more nuts is connected with decreases in both weight and waist circumference. The research included a large assortment of nuts—including cashews, pistachios, almonds, walnuts, and peanuts (8).

Additionally, a daily intake of a handful or approximately 50g of nuts can lower LDL-cholesterol levels (1). Try to incorporate a wide variety of nuts and seeds such as peanuts, pistachios, walnuts, hazelnuts, pecans, cashews, etc. for a more diverse nutrient profile.

If whole nuts are not your thing, try nut butter instead. Two tablespoons of nut butter is a serving. Remember to choose unsalted nuts and no salt-added nut butter to manage your daily sodium intake.

How does it work? Nuts are rich in unsaturated fats, particularly monounsaturated and polyunsaturated fats, which are known to reduce LDL cholesterol. These healthy fats help to improve the health of the arteries by reducing inflammation and oxidative stress.

Impact on Cholesterol: Studies have shown that consuming nuts regularly can lead to a modest decrease in LDL cholesterol levels. Choosing a variety of nuts in the diet ensures a broad range of nutrients and healthy fats that contribute to this effect.

Types: Almonds, walnuts, pistachios, pecans, and hazelnuts are particularly beneficial.

Benefits: Nuts are rich in unsaturated fats, which help lower "bad" LDL-cholesterol levels and reduce the risk of heart disease. They also provide essential nutrients like vitamin E, magnesium, and potassium.

Nutrient Profile: High in monounsaturated and polyunsaturated fats, protein, fiber, vitamin E, magnesium, and other minerals. Nuts are calorie-dense, so portion control is important.

Daily Serving: A small handful of nuts (about 50 grams) per day is recommended in the Portfolio Diet. It's important to consume them raw or dry-roasted without added salts or sugars.

3. Plant Protein

Compared to animal-based protein, plant-based protein can provide more fiber which we have discussed as its benefits above, and contain more healthy fats that regulate cholesterol levels (7).

To consume the recommended daily intake of 50 grams of plant protein, you should explore various options including legumes, pulses, nuts, seeds, and whole grains (6). Minimally processed soy protein includes soybean, tofu, tempeh, natto, and miso are beneficial too.

How Does It Work: Plant proteins are effective in lowering cholesterol primarily due to two key factors: their high soluble fiber content and low levels of saturated fat. Soluble fiber helps reduce the absorption of cholesterol into the bloodstream. This type of fiber binds with cholesterol in the digestive system and aids in its excretion from the body. Additionally, plant proteins are typically low in saturated fats, which are known to increase LDL ('bad') cholesterol levels when consumed in excess.

Impact on Cholesterol: By replacing animal proteins, which are higher in saturated fats, with plant-based proteins, individuals can significantly reduce their intake of saturated fats that contribute to higher LDL cholesterol levels, thereby promoting better heart health.

Food Sources: Tofu, tempeh, unsweetened soy beverage, beans, peas, legumes, nuts, seeds, seitan, nuts and seed butters are a few.

Benefits: Plant protein can lower LDL cholesterol and provides a high-quality source of plant-based protein. Soy protein is also rich in isoflavones, which have been linked to various health benefits.

Nutrient Profile: They offer not only high-quality protein but also a wealth of essential nutrients like fiber, healthy unstaurated fats, vitamins (including B vitamins and Vitamin E), and minerals (such as iron, magnesium, and zinc). These foods are also characterized by their low levels of saturated fats.

Daily Intake Goal: Incorporate around 50 grams of plant protein into your daily diet.

4. Plant Sterols

Plant sterols, or phytosterols, have similar chemical structures compared to cholesterol. They can block the absorption of cholesterol, preventing it from entering the bloodstream and remaining in our digestive system, to be removed as waste (9).

How Does It Work? Plant sterols have a structure similar to cholesterol, which allows them to effectively block the absorption of cholesterol in the intestines. By competing with cholesterol for absorption, they reduce the amount of cholesterol that enters the bloodstream.

Food Sources: Vegetables, fruits, vegetable oils, nuts and seeds, legumes, whole grains, fortified foods and supplements

Benefits: Plant sterols, or phytosterols, are beneficial for heart health as they lower LDL cholesterol, potentially reduce inflammation and cancer risks, and may support the immune system, all of which contribute to their role in a balanced, heart-healthy diet.

Nutrient Profile: Foods high in plant sterols, like nuts, seeds, and unsaturated fat oils, are not only valued for cholesterol-lowering effects but also provide essential nutrients such as fiber, healthy unsaturated fats, vitamins E and K, B-complex vitamins, and minerals like magnesium and potassium.

Daily Intake Goal: Phytosterols occur naturally in some fruits and vegetables but to reach the daily recommended intake of 2 grams, explore fortified options such as spreads, yogurt, and cereals (6). Some may opt for dietary supplements.

Other Considerations

Eating Out

Eating out can definitely be a challenge when you are trying to be conscious of your diet. However, that does not mean you can't enjoy a night out on the town.

When you are eating out try to look for dishes that contain loads of vegetables and plant-based proteins such as tofu, chickpea, and lentils. Be sure to avoid options that are high in saturated and trans fat such as deep-fried foods.

Do not hesitate to talk to the restaurant staff about the ingredients of a dish so you can make an informed decision.

Nut Allergy

For individuals with nut allergies, seeds offer a nutritious and safe alternative within the Portfolio Diet.

Seeds such as chia, flaxseed, hemp, pumpkin and sunflower are not only versatile in their use but also rich in many of the same beneficial nutrients found in nuts, including essential fatty acids, proteins, and fibers. These seeds can be easily incorporated into various meals, from sprinkling on salads and yogurt to blending into smoothies or baking into whole-grain breads.

However, it's crucial to recognize that dietary changes, especially when managing allergies and specific health goals like cholesterol reduction, should be approached with expert guidance. Consulting with a Registered Dietitian ensures that your modified Portfolio Diet remains balanced, nutritious, and tailored to your individual health needs.

A dietitian can provide personalized advice on portion sizes, suggest additional nutrient-rich foods to complement your diet, and help you navigate the challenges of maintaining a diverse and heart-healthy diet without nuts. This professional guidance is invaluable in ensuring that your dietary choices effectively contribute to your overall health and well-being.

Soy Allergy

For individuals who are allergic to soy or prefer to avoid it, the Portfolio Diet can still be effectively adapted using alternative plant-based protein sources. Foods such as lentils, chickpeas, beans, quinoa, and seitan are excellent substitutes, offering not only high protein content but also other beneficial nutrients like fiber, vitamins, and minerals. Research in nutritional science supports the use of diverse plant-based proteins in managing cholesterol levels and promoting heart health.

Studies have shown that diets rich in various plant proteins can contribute to lowering LDL (bad) cholesterol, similar to the effects observed with soy protein. This is particularly encouraging for those with dietary restrictions, as it provides flexibility and inclusivity in dietary planning (7).

It's important, however, to consult with a Registered Dietitian when making these substitutions. A dietitian can help ensure that your diet remains balanced and nutritionally adequate, providing tailored advice on how to integrate a variety of plant-based proteins into your meals effectively. This professional guidance is crucial in making informed dietary choices that align with your health goals and dietary needs, ensuring that the absence of soy doesn't hinder the efficacy of the Portfolio Diet in managing cholesterol and promoting overall well-being.

Get Started with Easy Swaps & Substitutions

The following are suggestions for substitutions that you can make if you're interested in switching to The Portfolio eating pattern.

- **Butter** – Fortified plant sterol margarine or nut butter like natural unsalted almond butter
- **Cow milk** – Unsweetened soy milk offers plant based protein
- **Burger beef patty** – Veggie, legume or soy patty for more plant based protein
- **Ground meat** – Tofu, tempeh or lentils adds plant based protein
- **Eggs** – Tofu scramble provides plant based protein
- **Animal-based cheese** – Nutritional yeast or nut-based cheese
- **Chips –** Nuts ,a key component of the Portfolio Diet
- **Couscous –** Quinoa is a complete plant protein
- **Sugary Cereals –** Oats are a great source of soluble fiber
- **Granola –** Chia seeds are a great source of soluble fiber
- **Mayonnaise –** Avocado provides healthy fats and fiber
- **Creamy Dips –** Hummus is plant-based, rich in protein and fiber
- **Salty Snacks –** Steamed edamame offers soy protein and fiber
- **Cream Cheese –** Almond butter provides healthy fats and protein
- **Croutons –** Try pumpkin seeds for crunch with more nutrients

A Summary

It is important to note that other aspects besides your diet can influence your cholesterol level, including physical activity level, stress, sleep, and medication. To maximize the cholesterol-lowering effect, try your best to maintain a healthy lifestyle.

Nuts - 50 grams/day

Source of healthy fats
Lowers LDL-cholesterol ("bad" cholesterol)

Almonds

Walnuts

Nut Butters

Pistachio

Soluble Viscous Fiber - 10-25 grams/day

Trap LDL-cholesterol in the digestive tract
Lower rate of cholesterol production in the liver

Whole grains

Vegetable & fruits

Legumes

Soy or Plant Protein - 50 grams/day

Sources of healthy fats and fiber compared to animal protein
Can raise HDL-cholesterol ("good" cholesterol)

Soybeans

Legumes like black beans, kidney beans, chickpeas

Tofu

Plant Sterols - 2 grams/day

Block absorption of cholesterol
Prevent cholesterol from entering the bloodstream
Opt for fortified options or supplements

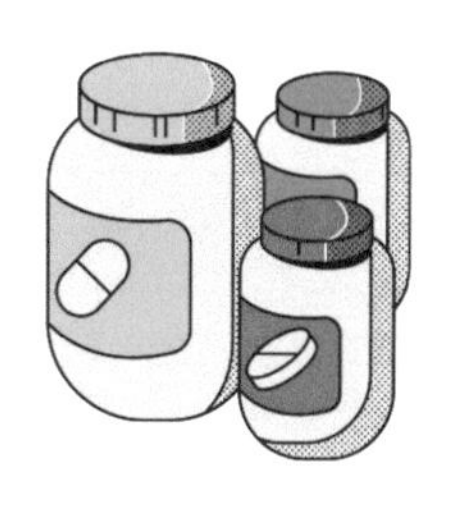

Vegetable Oils

Fortified Foods

Supplements

Are You Eating The Portfolio Way?

Answer the questions about your eating habits to know if you are eating The Portfolio Eating Pattern (10). If you answer “no” to any question, think of a way you can move that “no” to a “yes” to get one step closer to eating The Portfolio way,

Question		
1. Do you eat nuts such as almonds, walnuts, and pecans each day?	☐ YES	☐ NO
2. Do you eat plant protein like fortified soy beverage, beans and legumes each day?	☐ YES	☐ NO
3. Do you eat foods higher in soluble viscous fiber such as barley, oats, and avocado each day?	☐ YES	☐ NO
4. Do you eat foods with plant sterols such as fortified margarine or take a plant sterol supplement each day?	☐ YES	☐ NO
5. Do you have beans, lentils, and peas at least 3 times a week?	☐ YES	☐ NO
6. Do you have vegetables and fruit at most meals and snacks?	☐ YES	☐ NO

Sources of Viscous Soluble Fiber

Since soluble fiber isn't on the nutrition facts table, I've included a reference table below to help you meet your daily goal of 10 to 25 grams per day.

Souce	Serving Size	Amount of grams (g)
Grains		
Psyllium seeds (ground)	1 tbsp	5 g
Barley, cooked	1/2 cup	4.1 g
Brain Buds	1/3 cup	3 g
Oatmeal, cooked	1/2 cup	2 g
Oat bran, cooked	3/4 cup	2 g
Whole grain bread	1 slice	1-3 g
Quinoa, cooked	1/2 cup	1.7 g
Vegetables		
Artichoke, cooked	1 medium	4.7 g
Green peas, cooked	1/2 cup	3.2 g
Sweet potato with skin	1 medium	2.7 g
Potato with skin	1 medium	2.4 g
Kale cooked	1 cup	2.1 g
Asparagus, cooked	1/2 cup	1.7 g
Brussels sprouts, cooked	1 cup	1.7 g
Zucchini, cooked	1/2 cup	1.4 g

Fruits		
Pear	1 large	3 g
Figs, dried	3 medium	3 g
Orange	1 medium	2.1 g
Kiwi	1 large	2.4 g
Avocado	1/2	2.0 g
Apricots, dried	4 medium	1.8 g
Raspberries	1 cup	1.8 g
Strawberries	1 cup	1.8 g
Prunes	4 medium	1.3 g
Beans		
Pinto beans, cooked	1/2 cup	5.5 g
Black beans, cooked	1/2 cup	3.8 g
Kidney beans, cooked	1/2 cup	3 g
Lima beans, cooked	1/2 cup,	3 g
Lentils, cooked	1/2 cup	3 g
Navy beans, cooked	1/2 cup	2 g
Edamame, cooked	1/2 cup	1.5 g
Chickpeas, cooked	1/2 cup	1 g
Nuts & Seeds		
Psyllium Seeds	2 tbsp	7.1 g
Metamucil	1 Tbsp	3.4 g
Flaxseed (ground)	2 tbsp	3 g
Peanuts	1 oz	1.1 g
Peanut Butter	2 tbsp	1.1 g
Sunflower Seeds	1/4 cup	1.1 g
Almonds	1 oz	0.7 g
Chia Seeds	1 Tbsp	0.7 g

Data retrieved from USDA FoodData Central and Canadian Nutrient File

Soluble viscous fiber (Aim for at least 10 grams a day)		
Each serving below has 2-3 grams of soluble fiber. Aim for 5 or more Servings a day		
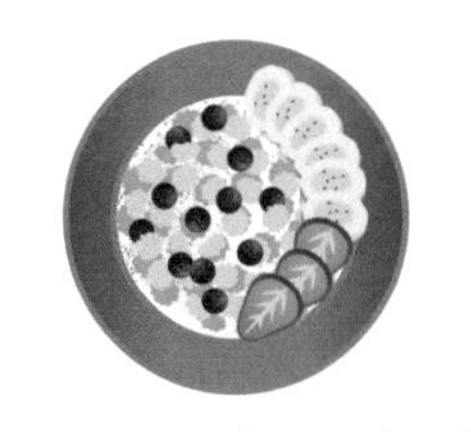 Oatmeal, cooked (2/3 cup/150 mL)	 Barley, cooked (1 1/3 cup/325 mL)	  Cereal with added psyllium or Psyllium husk (1/4 cup/60 mL)

Tips to eat soluble viscous fiber

- Have a bowl of oatmeal for breakfast with a pear
- Instead of rice or quinoa at a meal try cooking barley.
- Sprinkle psyllium husk or oats to your cereals soups, yogurt, baked goods or add to your smoothies recipes.
- Make snacks count by eating soluble fiber rich fruits and vegetables
- Ask your health care professional about using a soluble viscous fiber supplement.

Other foods higher in soluble viscous fiber

- Choose produce like pears, nectarines, apples, orange, eggplant, okra and avocados more often.
- Eat dried cooked legumes, beans, peas, and lentils at a minimum of 3 times a week. Add them to casseroles, soups, stir fries and chili.

Sources of Plant Protein

Since plant protein isn't on the nutrition facts table, I've included a reference table below to help you meet your daily goal of 50 grams of plant protein per day.

Souce	Serving Size	Amount of grams (g)
Tempeh	1/2 cup	16 g
Tofu, firm	1/4 cup (60 grams)	10 g
Edamame, frozen	1/2 cup	12 g
Soy beverage	1 cup	7 g
Lentils, cooked	1/2 cup	9g
Quinoa, cooked	1 cup	8 g
Beans (black, kidney, navy)	1/2 cup	7 g
Pumpkin seeds	1/4 cup	11 g
Hemp seeds	3 tbsp	9 g
Soy protein powder	1 scoop	15-30 g

Data retrieved from USDA FoodData Central and Canadian Nutrient File

Sources of plant based protein

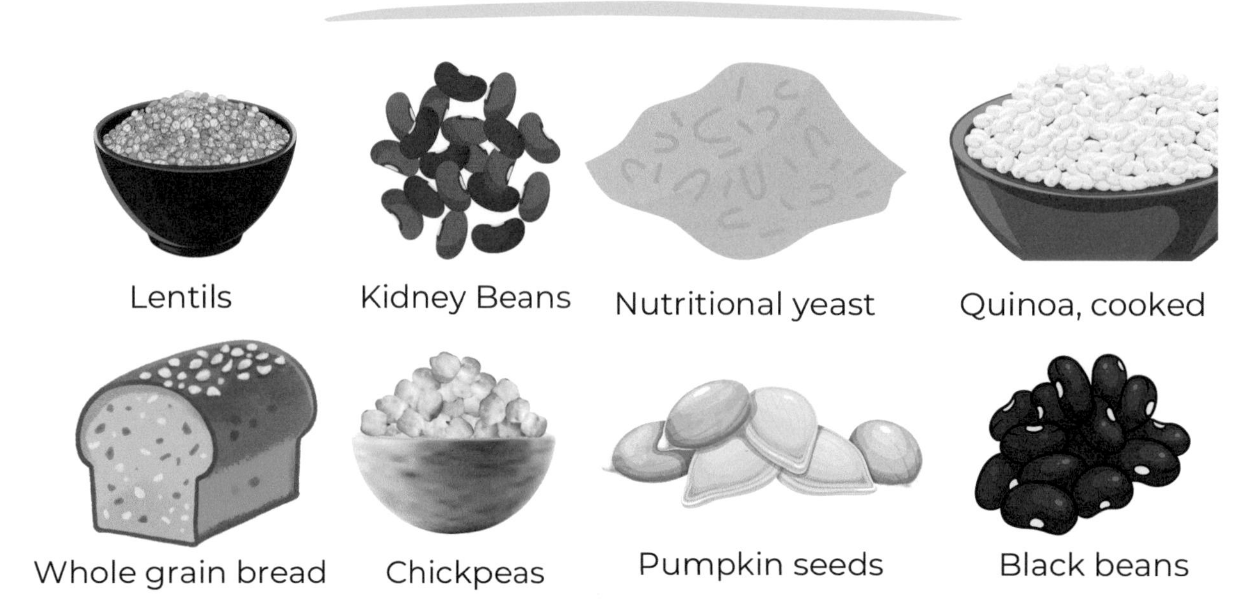

Plant Protein (Aim for at least 50 grams a day)

Each serving below has 2-3 grams of soluble fiber. Aim for 5 or more Servings a day

Unsweetened soy beverage (1 cup or 250 mL)	Nuts and seeds (1/4 cup or 60 mL	Tempeh, miso, natto (1/3 cup or 75 mL)	Tofu: Firm (1/2 cup or 125 mL) & Soft (3/4 cup or 175 mL)	Edamame beans, shelled (1/2 cup or 125 mL)	Beans and legumes (1/2 cup or 125 mL)	Soy protein powder supplement (1.5 tbsp or 20 mL)

Tips to eat more plant protein

- Instead of cow's milk, try drinking unsweetened soy beverage. Have a glass with meals or snack.
- Incorporate soy beverage into your morning cereal, as well as in your coffee-based lattes or baked goods.
- Enhance your smoothies by adding tofu, unsweetened soy beverage , beans, legumes, nuts, seeds or soy protein powder for an extra protein boost.
- For a healthy snack, reach for roasted chickpeas or edamame beans.
- Aim for at least one meatless meal per week. Add beans, tofu, and lentils to casseroles, soups, stir fries and chili.
- Try topping your cereal, salads, yogurt with nuts and seeds.

Sample Meal Plans

This is a sample Portfolio Diet meal plan that you can either follow or customize based on your personal preference!

Day One

- **Breakfast:** overnight oat bran (recipe on page 58) with walnuts, blueberries and 1 cup of unsweetened soy beverage - *contains soluble fiber, plant protein, nuts, plant sterols*
- **Lunch:** tofu scramble (recipe on page 90) with eggplant on oat bran toast, served with a pear - *contains soluble fiber, plant protein, nuts, plant sterols*
- **Dinner:** lentil burrito (recipe on page 73) with carrot sticks, sliced red peppers and 1 cup of unsweetened soy beverage - *contains soluble fiber, plant protein, nuts, plant sterols*
- **Snack:** banana flaxseed pudding (recipe on page 60) - *contains soluble fiber, plant protein, nuts, plant sterols*

Day Two

- **Breakfast:** peanut butter avocado toast (recipe on page 72) on oat bran bread with one cup of unsweetened soy beverage and a plum - *contains soluble fiber, plant protein, nuts, plant sterols*
- **Lunch:** Mediterranean chickpea quinoa bowl (recipe on page 74) served with 1 cup of unsweetened soy beverage - *contains soluble fiber, plant protein, nuts, plant sterols*
- **Dinner:** curried potato and pea stew served (page 99) with roasted parsnip and a pear for dessert - *contains soluble fiber, plant protein, plant sterols*
- **Snack:** a lentil muffin (recipe on page 106) with an apple - *contains soluble fiber, plant protein, nuts, plant sterols*

Day Three

- **Breakfast**: tofu toast (recipe on page 71) on oat bread served with one cup of unsweetened soy beverage and a peach - *contains soluble fiber, plant protein, nuts, plant sterols*
- **Lunch**: tomato oatmeal soup (recipe on page 76) with one cup of unsweetened soy beverage and 1 cup of strawberries - *contains soluble fiber, plant sterols, nuts*
- **Dinner**: spaghetti sauce with lentils (recipe on page 91) a salad and 1 cup of unsweetened soy beverage - *contains soluble fiber, plant protein, plant sterols*
- **Snack**: peanut butter banana smoothie (recipe on page 49) - *contains soluble fiber, plant protein, nuts, plant sterols*

Day Four

- **Breakfast:** apple spice baked oats (recipe on page 61) with one cup of unsweetened soy beverage and a plum - *contains soluble fiber, plant protein, nuts, plant sterols*
- **Lunch:** Mediterranean hummus toast (recipe on page 82) on oat bread with 1 cup of unsweetened soy beverage and one pear - *contains soluble fiber, plant protein, seeds, plant sterols*
- **Dinner:** warm sweet potato lentil salad (recipe on page 96) - *contains soluble fiber, plant protein, plant sterols*
- **Snack:** prune banana bread (page 120) - *contains soluble fiber, plant protein, nuts, plant sterols*

Day Five

- **Breakfast**: cookie dough baked oats (recipe on page 59) and one cup of unsweetened soy beverage and a apple - *contains soluble fiber, plant protein, plant sterols*
- **Lunch**: heart healthy chili (recipe on page 83) with corn chips - *contains soluble fiber, plant protein, plant sterols*
- **Dinner**: heart healthy pizza (recipe on page 95) and one cup of unsweetened soy beverage - *contains soluble fiber, plant protein, plant sterols*
- **Snack**: quick chickpea salad (recipe on page 115) and a handful of dried apricots - *contains soluble fiber, plant protein, plant sterols*

Smoothies

Chia Seed Coffee

2 Servings

Prep Time: 10 minutes

Cook Time: 20 minutes

Total Time: 30 minutes

Ingredients

- 3 tbsp chia seeds
- ¼ cup room temperature water
- 2 tsp instant coffee
- ½ cup hot water
- 1 cup soy milk (unsweetened)
- 1 tsp cinnamon

Instructions

- Bloom chia seeds in room temperature water for 20 minutes.
- Combine instant coffee and hot water in a bowl.
- Blend milk into the coffee mixture until creamy.
- Drain chia seeds to remove extra water.
- Stir bloomed chia seeds into coffee.
- Pour into a glass, sprinkle cinnamon, and enjoy!

Lower Cholesterol Smoothie

2 Servings

Prep Time: 5 minutes

Cook Time: 0 minutes

Total Time: 5 minutes

Ingredients

- ⅓ large flake oats
- 2 tbsp flaxseed (ground)
- ⅓ cup spinach (packed)
- 2 tbsp almond butter
- ⅓ cup blueberries
- ½ tsp cinnamon
- ½ avocado
- 1 cup soy milk (unsweetened)

Instructions

- In a blender combine all ingredients and blend until smooth.
- Adjust consistency by adding milk or water to preferred consistency.
- Serve and enjoy!

Chocolate Avocado Smoothie

1 Servings

Prep Time: 5 minutes

Cook Time: 5 minutes

Total Time: 10 minutes

Ingredients

- 4 tbsp large flake oats
- 1 cup soy milk (unsweetened)
- 1 banana (frozen)
- ½ avocado
- 1 tbsp peanut butter (natural)
- 1 tsp cocoa powder

Instructions

- Soak oats in milk for 30 mins before blending (optional).
- Blend all ingredients until smooth; add milk as needed for desired consistency.
- Serve while cold and enjoy!

Creamy Avocado Peanut Butter Smoothie

1 Serving

Prep Time: 5 minutes

Cook Time: 5 minutes

Total Time: 10 minutes

Ingredients

- 1 banana
- ½ avocado
- 2 tbsp cocoa powder
- ¼ plain Greek yogurt
- 1 ½ peanut butter
- 1 cup soy milk (unsweetened)
- 2-3 dates (pitted)

Instructions

- Blend banana, avocado, cocoa powder, yogurt, peanut butter, soy milk, and dates.
- Blend until smooth.
- Pour and enjoy!

Pea Smoothie

- 1 Servings
- Prep Time: 5 minutes
- Cook Time: 0 minutes
- Total Time: 5 minutes

Ingredients

- 1 banana
- ½ cup green peas (frozen)
- ½ cup spinach
- 1 tsp chia seeds
- 1 date (pitted)
- ⅓ cup greek yogurt
- 1 cup soy milk (unsweetened)

Instructions

- In a blender add all ingredients together.
- Blend until smooth.
- Serve cold and enjoy!

Red Bean Smoothie

- 2 Servings
- Prep Time: 5 minutes
- Cook Time: 0 minutes
- Total Time: 5 minutes

Ingredients

- ½ cup canned red kidney beans (drained & rinsed)
- 1 cup frozen pitted cherries
- ½ cup spinach
- 1 cup soy milk (unsweetened)
- 3 dates (pitted)

Instructions

- Add all ingredients into a blender and pulse until. completely smooth.
- Serve while cold and enjoy!

White Bean Smoothie

1 serving

Prep Time: 5 minutes

Cook Time: 0 minutes

Total Time: 5 minutes

Ingredients

- ⅓ cup canned white kidney beans (drained and rinsed)
- 1 tbsp flaxseed (ground)
- ½ cup peaches (frozen)
- ½ cup mangoes (frozen)
- 1 cup soy milk (unsweetened)
- 1 date (pitted)

Instructions

- In a blender add all of the ingredients together.
- Blend until smooth.
- Serve cold and enjoy!

Homemade Juice

 3 Servings

Prep Time: 20 minutes

Cook Time: 0 minutes

Total Time: 20 minutes

Ingredients

- 2 tbsp chia seeds
- ¼ cup water (for chia seeds)
- 2 mangoes (medium)
- ¾ cup soy milk (unsweetened)

Instructions

- Soak chia seeds in room temperature water for 20 mins to bloom, stirring to ensure all seeds are covered.
- Blend chopped mangoes, and milk until smooth.
- In a glass, add a scoop of bloomed chia seeds.
- Pour mango juice over chia seeds.
- Enjoy!

Chocolate Banana Smoothie

1 Servings

Prep Time: 5 minutes

Cook Time: 0 minutes

Total Time: 5 minutes

Ingredients

- ½ cup old fashioned oats
- 1 banana
- 1 tsp cacao powder
- 1 tbsp almond butter
- 1 medjool date (pitted)
- 1 cup soy milk (unsweetened)

Instructions

- Pulse oats in a blender for a fine texture.
- Add all remaining ingredients into blender. Blitz until smooth and enjoy!

Peanut Butter Banana Smoothie

1 Serving

Prep Time: 5 minutes

Cook Time: 5 minutes

Total Time: 10 minutes

Ingredients

- ¼ cup soy milk (unsweetened)
- ¼ cup old fashioned oats
- 2 tbsp peanut butter (organic)
- 1 large banana (sliced)
- 1 tsp cinnamon
- ⅓ cup greek yogurt
- 1 tsp chia seeds

Instructions

- In a blender add all ingredients together.
- Adjust consistency to liking by adding more or less milk.
- Serve cold and enjoy!

Peanut Butter Cup Smoothie

1 Servings

Prep Time: 5 minutes

Cook Time: 0 minutes

Total Time: 5 minutes

Ingredients

- 1 banana
- 1 tbsp cacao powder
- 1 tbsp peanut butter
- 1 tbsp maple syrup
- 1 tsp flaxseed
- 1 tsp hemp seed
- 1 cup soy milk (unsweetened)

Instructions

- In a blender add all ingredients together.
- Adjust consistency to liking by adding more or less milk.
- Serve cold and enjoy!

Watermelon Tofu Smoothie

1 serving

Prep Time: 5 minutes

Cook Time: 5 minutes

Total Time: 10 minutes

Ingredients

- ½ cup watermelon (sliced)
- ½ cup pineapple (chunks)
- ¼ cup strawberries (sliced)
- ½ cup soy milk (unsweetened)
- ½ cup tofu (cubed)

Instructions

- In a blender, add the watermelon, pineapple, strawberries, and soy milk.
- In the meantime, drain the soft and silken tofu from any excess water using a paper towel. Then, add the tofu.
- Blend until smooth.
- Serve and enjoy!

Breakfast

Barley Pancakes

- 4 Servings
- Prep Time: 15 minutes
- Cook Time: 15 minutes
- Total Time: 30 minutes

Ingredients

- 2 cups barley flour
- 1 tbsp baking powder
- ⅛ salt
- 3 tbsp maple syrup
- 1 egg
- 2 cups soy milk (unsweetened)
- 1 tbsp vanilla extract
- 3 tbsp extra virgin olive oil

Instructions

- Heat griddle, brush with olive oil.
- Whisk barley flour, baking powder, and salt.
- In a separate bowl, whisk maple syrup, egg, milk, vanilla, and olive oil.
- Combine wet and dry ingredients, avoiding over mixing.
- Ladle batter onto the griddle.
- Flip when bubbles appear, cook for 1-2 minutes and enjoy!

3 Ingredient Pancakes

4 Servings

Prep Time: 5 minutes

Cook Time: 10 minutes

Total Time: 15 minutes

Ingredients

- 1 ½ cup large flake oats
- 1 banana
- 1 cup soy milk (unsweetened)

Instructions

- Blitz oats in a blender until coarse flour consistency then add banana and milk. Blend to form smooth batter and allow batter to sit for 5-10 mins to thicken.
- Heat pan, grease with oil, pour ¼ cup batter per pancake onto pan.
- Cook until bubbles form and surface looks dry (2-3 mins).
- Flip, cook 1-2 mins until toasted, then keep warm.
- Top with desired toppings and enjoy warm!

Brownie Baked Oats

6 Servings

Prep Time: 10 minutes

Cook Time: 45 minutes

Total Time: 55 minutes

Ingredients

- 2 cup old fashioned oats
- ½ cocoa powder
- ¾ baking powder
- ¼ salt
- ⅓ brown sugar
- 2 tbsp flaxseed (ground)
- 2 cup soy milk (unsweetened)
- ⅔ applesauce (no sugar added)
- ¼ dark chocolate chip

Instructions

- Preheat oven to 375°F and grease an 8×8 baking dish.
- Mix oats, cocoa, baking powder, salt, sugar, flaxseeds.
- Add soy milk and applesauce to the dry ingredients, mixing evenly.
- Pour the mixture into dish and smooth it over.
- Top with chocolate chips.
- Bake for 45-55 minutes until the middle is set.
- Cool 5-10 mins before enjoying!

Vegan Protein Oatmeal

- 4 Servings
- Prep Time: 5 minutes
- Cook Time: 30 minutes
- Total Time: 35 minutes

Ingredients

- 3 cups water
- ¼ salt
- ½ cup red lentils (sorted and rinsed)
- 1 cup steel cut oats
- 1½ cup soy milk (unsweetened)
- ¼ cup pumpkin puree
- 1 tsp pumpkin pie spice
- ¼ cup walnuts (optional)

Instructions

- Bring water, salt, lentils, and oats to a boil; stir.
- Reduce heat, add milk, and stir.
- Cover, cook for 25-30 mins until lentils and oats are done, stirring occasionally.
- Add pumpkin and nuts.
- Enjoy!

Overnight Oat Bran

1 Serving

Prep Time: 5 minutes

Cook Time: 2 hours

Total Time: 2 hours and 5 minutes

Ingredients

- ⅓ oat bran
- ⅔ cup soy milk (unsweetened)
- 1 tbsp almond butter
- 2 tbsp hemp seed
- ½ tsp cinnamon

Instructions

- Add your oat bran, milk, and any optional toppings into a jar like almond butter, hemp seed and cinnamon.
- Stir well.
- Pop a lid on the jar and place it in the refrigerator.
- Refrigerate for at least 2 hours, then enjoy.

Cookie Dough Baked Oats

6 Servings

Prep Time: 15 minutes

Cook Time: 55 minutes

Total Time: 1 hour 10 minutes

Ingredients

- 1 medium ripe banana
- 2 eggs
- 1 tsp vanilla
- ⅓ almond butter
- 2 tbsp maple syrup
- ¾ cup soy milk (unsweetened)
- 2 cups old fashioned oats
- 1 tsp baking powder
- ½ cinnamon
- ¼ semi-sweet chocolate chips

Instructions

- Preheat oven to 350°F and grease an 8x8 baking dish.
- Mash banana in a bowl, add eggs, vanilla, almond butter, maple syrup, and soy milk. Whisk until combined.
- Add oats, baking powder and cinnamon, mix well.
- Pour into dish, spread, top with chocolate chips.
- Bake 25-30 mins until toothpick comes out clean.
- Cool 15 mins, cut into 9 squares.
- Top with nut butter or enjoy with yogurt and berries if desired!

Banana Flaxseed Pudding

1 Serving

Prep Time: 5 minutes

Cook Time: 2 hours

Total Time: 2 hour 5 minutes

Ingredients

- ½ banana (mashed)
- ¼ flaxseed (ground)
- ¾ cup soy milk (unsweetened)
- ¾ tsp cinnamon (ground)
- ¼ tsp vanilla extract
- ¼ cup walnuts (chopped)

Instructions

- Mash half the banana in a bowl.
- In another bowl, combine flaxseed, milk, cinnamon, vanilla, and walnuts.
- Add mashed banana to flaxseed mixture.
- Refrigerate for at least 2 hours, then enjoy.

Apple Spice Baked Oats

4 Servings

Prep Time: 10 minutes

Cook Time: 45 minutes

Total Time: 55 minutes

Ingredients

- 2 cups old fashioned oats
- 1 tsp baking powder
- ⅛ salt
- 1 tsp cinnamon
- 1 tsp pumpkin pie spice
- ⅓ cup brown sugar
- 2 tbsp flaxseed (ground)
- 2 cups soy milk (unsweetened)
- 1 tsp extra virgin olive oil
- ⅔ cup applesauce
- 1 apple (cored and diced with skin on)
- ½ walnuts (chopped)

Instructions

- Preheat oven to 375°F and grease 8x8 dish with olive oil.
- In a bowl, add oats, baking powder, salt, cinnamon, pumpkin pie spice, brown sugar, flaxseed and mix.
- Add milk, olive oil and applesauce to dry ingredients, stir until well incorporated.
- Gently fold in diced apple and chopped walnuts.
- Pour into baking dish, top with chopped walnuts, bake for 45 minutes until golden. Cool for 5-10 minutes, enjoy warm!

Blueberry Cheesecake Overnight Oats

1 Serving

Prep Time: 10 minutes

Cook Time: 2 hour

Total Time: 2 hour 10 minutes

Ingredients

- 2 tbsp steel cut oats
- ½ tsp honey (crust)
- ¼ tsp cinnamon
- 1 tsp almond butter
- 1 tsp soy milk (crust)
- ½ cup old fashioned oats
- ¼ cup soy milk (unsweetened)
- 1 tbsp flaxseed (ground)
- 1 tsp honey
- ½ vanilla
- ¼ cup plain Greek yogurt
- 1 tbsp cream cheese
- ½ cup blueberries

Instructions

- To make the crust, mix steel-cut oats, honey, cinnamon, almond butter, and soy milk in a small bowl. Press the mixture into the bottom of a jar or container.
- Blend oats, milk, flaxseed, honey, vanilla, yogurt, and cream cheese until smooth for the oatmeal cheesecake mixture.
- Pour oat mixture over the crust, and add blueberries on top.
- Chill in the fridge for at least 2 hours or overnight to thicken.

Pecan Pie Overnight Oats

- 1 Serving
- Prep Time: 5 minutes
- Cook Time: 2 hour
- Total Time: 2 hour 5 minutes

Ingredients

- ½ cup old fashioned oats
- 1 tsp flaxseed (ground)
- 2 tbsp pecans (chopped)
- ¾ tsp cinnamon
- ⅛ tsp nutmeg
- 1 tbsp almond butter
- 2 tsp maple Syrup
- ½ tsp vanilla extract
- ½ cup soy milk (unsweetened)
- ⅓ cup Greek yogurt
- 2 tbsp pecans & ½ tsp cinnamon (optional)

Instructions

- Combine oats, ground flaxseed, pecans, cinnamon, and nutmeg in a bowl; stir well.
- Add almond butter, maple syrup, vanilla extract, and soy milk; mix until combined.
- Transfer mixture to a jar, top with Greek yogurt.
- Sprinkle additional pecans and cinnamon on top.
- Chill in the fridge for at least 2 hours or overnight.

Chia Banana Bread

12 Servings

Prep Time: 15 minutes

Cook Time: 45 minutes

Total Time: 1 hour

Ingredients

- ¾ soy milk (unsweetened)
- 1 tbsp apple cider vinegar
- 2 cup all purpose flour
- 1 tsp baking soda
- ½ tsp salt
- 1 tsp cinnamon
- ¾ maple syrup
- 2 eggs
- 1 tsp lemon zest
- 1 tsp vanilla
- ½ cup avocado oil
- 3 bananas (ripe)
- ¼ cup chia seeds
- ½ cup walnuts (chopped)

Instructions

- Preheat oven to 350°F.
- Whisk soy milk and vinegar in a measuring cup; let sit for 5-10 mins to thicken.
- In a large bowl, whisk flour, baking soda, salt, and cinnamon.

Chia Banana Bread

Instructions Continued

- In another bowl, whisk soy milk mixture, maple syrup, eggs, lemon zest, and vanilla. Add mashed banana, chia seeds and milk mixture; combine into a thick batter.
- Slowly pour the flour mixture into the banana mixture; fold with a spatula, avoiding overmixing.
- Grease a 9x3x5 inch loaf pan, pour in batter, and top with walnuts.
- Bake for 45-50 minutes; use a toothpick to check for doneness.
- Allow to cool before slicing. Enjoy!

Steel Cut Oat Granola

8 Servings

Prep Time: 10 minutes

Cook Time: 18 minutes

Total Time: 28 minutes

Ingredients

- 2 cups steel cut oats
- 1 cup pecans (chopped)
- 2½ tsp cinnamon
- ⅛ tsp salt
- 3 tbsp flaxseed (ground)
- 2 tsp vanilla
- ¼ cup maple syrup
- ¼ cup almond butter
- ¼ cup extra virgin olive oil

Instructions

- Preheat oven to 325°F and line a baking sheet with parchment paper.
- Combine steel-cut oats, chopped nuts, cinnamon, salt, and ground flaxseed in a bowl; stir.
- In a small dish, mix vanilla, maple syrup, almond butter, and oil until combined.
- Add wet ingredients to the bowl with dry ingredients; fold until thoroughly mixed.
- Transfer granola to baking sheet, spread to about 1cm thickness, and press down.
- Bake for 18-20 minutes until golden.
- Allow to cool completely on the baking sheet for big clusters.

Oat Bran Pancakes

1 Serving

Prep Time: 5 minutes

Cook Time: 10 minutes

Total Time: 15 minutes

Ingredients

- 2 egg
- 1/4th cup Greek yogurt (plain)
- 1 tsp cinnamon
- 1 tbsp flaxseed (ground)
- 1/2 cup oat bran
- 1 tsp extra virgin olive oil
- 1/2 cup strawberries
- 1/2 cup bananas

Instructions

- In a mixing bowl, whisk together the eggs, the yogurt, cinnamon, and ground flax. Add the oat bran and mix until a batter forms.
- Heat the oil in a pan over medium-high heat. Scoop 1/2 cup of batter at a time into the pan, and cook until bubbles start to form. Flip and cook for another one to two minutes. Repeat with the remaining batter.
- Plate the pancakes and top with the strawberries and bananas. Enjoy!

Lunch

Black Bean Toast with Avocado

2 Servings

Prep Time: 5 minutes

Cook Time: 0 minutes

Total Time: 5 minutes

Ingredients

- 2 slices whole grain bread
- 1 cup canned no salt added black beans (drained and rinsed)
- ½ avocado
- 2 tbsp water
- 1 tsp chili pepper flakes

Instructions

- Toast your bread of choice.
- Blend avocado and rinsed black beans until smooth, adding water gradually.
- Spread the mixture on the toast slices and garnish with chili peppers.

Tofu Toast

2 Servings

Prep Time: 5 minutes

Cook Time: 0 minutes

Total Time: 5 minutes

Ingredients

- 2 slices whole grain bread
- ⅓ block firm tofu
- 1 avocado
- 2 tbsp everything bagel spice

Instructions

- Toast your bread of choice.
- Crumble tofu in a small bowl using a fork.
- Smash or mash avocado in another bowl.
- Mix crumbled tofu and smashed avocado for a creamy spread.
- Spread the mixture on the toast slices and garnish with everything bagel spice.

Peanut Butter Avocado Toast

2 Servings

Prep Time: 5 minutes

Cook Time: 0 minutes

Total Time: 5 minutes

Ingredients

- 2 slices whole grain bread
- 1 avocado
- 3 tbsp natural peanut butter (smooth)
- ¼ cup sunflower seeds

Instructions

- Toast your bread of choice
- Mash avocado with a fork and mix in sunflower seeds.
- Spread peanut butter on bread, top with avocado mixture.
- Serve immediately.

Lentil Burrito

4 Servings

Prep Time: 10 minutes

Cook Time: 15 minutes

Total Time: 25 minutes

Ingredients

- 4 large tortillas
- 1 can(19 oz/540 mL) of no salt added lentils
- ½ cup pepitas
- 2 cloves garlic
- 1½ tsp chili powder
- 1½ tsp cumin
- ½ tsp oregano
- 1 tsp paprika
- 1 tbsp extra virgin olive oil
- 2 medium tomatoes
- 1 medium red onion
- 1 jalapeno pepper
- 1 tbsp lime juice
- Avocado

Instructions

- For the lentil filling, pulse (drained & rinsed) lentils, pepitas (roasted & unsalted), garlic, chili powder, cumin, oregano, paprika, and olive oil in a food processor for a textured mixture.
- Heat the mixture in a frying pan.
- For the salsa dice tomatoes, red onion, and jalapeño; combine with lime juice.
- Allow the salsa to marinate.
- To assemble the burrito, warm tortillas.
- Add mashed avocado, warm lentil filling, and tomato salsa to each tortilla.
- Top with Greek yogurt, and roasted pepitas.
- Roll up, serve warm, and enjoy!

Chickpea Quinoa Bowl

4 Servings

Prep Time: 10 minutes

Cook Time: 1 hour

Total Time: 1 hour 10 minutes

Ingredients

- 2 tbsp extra virgin olive oil
- 1 tsp chilli powder, 1 tsp garlic 1 tsp chaat masala, 2 tsp paprika
- 1 can (19 oz/540 mL) of no salt added chickpeas
- 1 sweet potato (diced)
- ½ tsp cinnamon
- 1 tsp brown sugar
- 2 tbsp tahini
- 2 tbsp cold water
- 1 tbsp cilantro (minced)
- ½ lime (juiced)
- ½ cup quinoa (rinsed)
- ½ cup carrots (sliced)
- 1 cup green peas (frozen)
- ½ cup cherry tomatoes (halved)

Instructions

- Preheat oven to 200F.
- Mix chili powder, garlic, chaat masala and paprika in a bowl.
- Coat chickpeas (drained & rinsed) in olive oil, add spice mixture, bake at 200 for 10 mins.
- Toss sweet potato in olive oil, cinnamor brown sugar; place on a baking sheet.
- Increase oven to 380F, bake sweet potato for 30-40 mins.
- Mix tahini, water, cilantro, and lime for dressing.
- Cook quinoa. Steam green peas and carrots on stove top.
- Assemble the dish: quinoa, roasted chickpeas, sweet potato, green peas, carrots and cherry tomatoes.
- Drizzle with dressing and enjoy!

Carrot Lentil Ginger Soup

4 Servings

Prep Time: 10 minutes

Cook Time: 30 minutes

Total Time:40 minutes

Ingredients

- 1 tbsp extra-virgin olive oil
- 4 large carrot (diced)
- 1 yellow onion (diced)
- 2 cloves garlic (minced)
- 2 tbsp ginger (ground)
- 1 tsp turmeric (ground)
- 1 cup dried red lentils
- 2 tbsp flaxseed (ground)
- 4 cups water
- 2 cups chicken broth (no salt added)

Instructions

- Heat olive oil in a stock pot on medium-high heat.
- Cook diced carrots and onion for around 5 mins or until caramelized.
- Add garlic, ground ginger, and turmeric; stir for 2 mins.
- Add red lentils, flaxseed, water, and chicken broth; stir and bring to a boil.
- Reduce heat, cover, and simmer for 20 mins until lentils and carrots are cooked.
- Remove from heat, use an immersion or kitchen blender to puree the soup.
- Pour into a bowl and enjoy!

Tomato Oatmeal Soup

- 4 Servings
- Prep Time: 5 minutes
- Cook Time: 25 minutes
- Total Time:30 minutes

Ingredients

- 1 tbsp extra virgin olive oil
- ½ medium yellow onion (diced)
- 1 large carrot (diced)
- 1 tsp garlic (minced)
- 1 tbsp tomato paste
- 4 cups vegetable broth (low sodium)
- ½ cup old fashioned oats
- 1 tsp black pepper
- 1 can (28 oz/ 830 mL) of diced no salt added tomatoes
- ¼ cup curly parsley (chopped)

Instructions

- Heat olive oil in a pot, add onion, carrot, and garlic; stir.
- Cover and cook on medium-low for 5-6 minutes, stirring occasionally.
- Add tomato paste, stir, and sauté for about 2-4 minutes.
- Add broth, oats, black pepper, and canned tomatoes with juices; simmer for 10-15 minutes until oats are cooked and broth thickens slightly.
- Remove from heat, stir in fresh parsley, and serve hot. Enjoy!

Protein Tomato Soup

6 Servings

Prep Time: 15 minutes

Cook Time: 30 minutes

Total Time:45 minutes

Ingredients

- 2 tbsp olive oil
- 3 large carrots (diced)
- 1 yellow onion (diced)
- 2 cloves garlic (minced)
- ¼ cup tomato paste (no salt added)
- 1 can (28 oz/ 830 mL) whole tomatoes
- 2 cups vegetable broth (no salt added)
- 2 tsp thyme
- 1 tbsp basil
- 1 cup Greek yogurt
- 1 cup white kidney beans
- ½ cup hemp seeds

Instructions

- Heat olive oil in a pot on medium heat.
- Add diced carrots, onion, and garlic; cook until vegetables are soft.
- Add tomato paste, cook for 30 seconds.
- Add whole peeled tomatoes, broth, thyme, and basil; stir.
- Cover and bring to a boil, then simmer for 15 minutes
- Add Greek yogurt, white kidney beans, and hemp seeds; mix well.
- Use an immersion blender to blend the soup into a smooth puree.
- Scoop into a bowl, sprinkle with nuts and sesame seeds if desired.

Greek Salad with Chickpeas

1 serving

Prep Time: 10 minutes

Cook Time: 0 minutes

Total Time: 10 minutes

Ingredients

- ¼ cup red onion (diced)
- ¾ cup canned no salt added chickpea (drained and rinsed)
- ½ cucumber (diced)
- 7 cherry tomatoes (halved)
- ⅕ cup olives (halved)
- Pinch of parsley leaves
- ¼ cup crumbled feta
- 1 tbsp lime juice
- 1 tbsp extra virgin olive oil
- black pepper to taste

Instructions

- In large bowl, combine onion, chickpeas, cucumber, cherry tomatoes, olives, parsley, feta, and toss well.
- Add lime juice, olive oil, add pepper to a small bowl, and stir to combine.
- Pour dressing over salad.
- Serve over leftover quinoa or barley.

Pulled Tofu Sandwich

- 2 Servings
- Prep Time: 5 minutes
- Cook Time: 15 minutes
- Total Time: 20 minutes

Ingredients

- ½ block extra firm tofu (grated)
- 4 slices whole wheat sourdough bread
- 1 tbsp extra virgin olive oil
- 1 tbsp garlic powder
- 1 tbsp paprika powder
- 1½ tbsp BBQ sauce
- 1 tomato (sliced)
- 1 cup spinach or any other leaves like lettuce, arugula, etc.
- 1 tbsp mayonnaise

Instructions

- Pat tofu to remove excess water, and grate gently with a cheese grater.
- Toast bread in the toaster,
- In a non-stick pan, heat olive oil and tofu on medium-high heat until golden.
- Sprinkle garlic and paprika on tofu.
- Keep frying until brown, or until crispy edges have formed.
- Add in BBQ sauce.
- Assemble the sandwich with cooked tofu, cucumber, tomato and leaves; adding mayonnaise as a condiment.

Corn and Lentil Soup

3 Servings

Prep Time: 10 minutes

Cook Time: 30 minutes

Total Time: 40 minutes

Ingredients

- 1 tbsp extra virgin olive oil
- 1 onion (diced)
- 3 cloves garlic (minced)
- 1.5 cups chicken broth (no salt added)
- 1.5 cups water
- ½ cup canned no salt added green lentils (drained and rinsed)
- 1 cup corn kernels
- 1 tomato (diced)
- 2 tsp oregano
- Black pepper
- Scallion or cilantro

Instructions

- Heat olive oil, sauté onion and garlic until fragrant.
- Add broth, water, and lentils; simmer covered for 10 minutes, stirring occasionally.
- Add corn, tomatoes, and oregano; simmer for another 15 minutes.
- Add black pepper to taste.
- Garnish with scallion or cilantro and serve!

Low Cholesterol Soup

4 Servings

Prep Time: 5 minutes

Cook Time: 36 minutes

Total Time: 45 minutes

Ingredients

- 4 tsp olive oil
- 1 white onion (chopped)
- 4 garlic cloves (minced)
- 1 tbsp Herbes de Provence
- ¾ cup barley
- 1 can (28 oz/830 mL) diced tomatoes, no salt added
- 1 can (19 oz/540 mL) no salt added cannellini beans
- 6 cup low sodium vegetable broth
- 2 cup spinach

Instructions

- Heat oil on medium-high heat in a large stockpot.
- Stir in onion, garlic, and Herbes de Provence and cook for around 5 minutes or until they turn golden.
- Add barley, tomatoes, beans and broth to the pot and stir until the soup comes to a boil. Lower the heat to medium, simmer the barley for approximately 15-20 minutes until cooked.
- Add the spinach and simmer for approximately one minute.

Mediterranean Hummus Toast

1 Serving

Prep Time: 5 minutes

Cook Time: 5 minutes

Total Time: 10 minutes

Ingredients

- 2 slices rye bread
- 1 garlic clove, minced
- 1/4 cup hummus
- 1/4 cup sunflower seeds
- 1/2 tsp oregano
- 1/2 tsp chili flakes

Instructions

- Toast the rye bread.
- To assemble, place the bread on plates.
- Spread garlic on both pieces of the toasted bread.
- Top each slice of bread evenly with the hummus, sunflower seeds, oregano and chili flakes. Enjoy!

Heart Healthy Chili

4 Servings

Prep Time: 10 minutes

Cook Time: 30 minutes

Total Time: 40 minutes

Ingredients

- 2 tbsp extra virgin olive oil
- 1 medium onion, diced
- 3 cloves garlic, minced
- 1 carrot, diced
- 1 jalapeno pepper, diced
- 2 tbsp tomato paste
- 1/4 cup water
- 1 can (28 oz/ 830 mL) low sodium diced tomatoes
- 1 can (19 oz/540 mL) no salt added six bean mix (drained and rinsed)
- 1 tbsp dried parsley, 1 tbsp dried oregano, 1 tbsp black pepper, 1 tbsp cumin and 1 tbsp paprika

Instructions

- To a pot add olive oil, onion, carrot, garlic, black pepper, cumin, and paprika. Cook on medium-high heat until the onions become transparent, stirring occasionally.
- Add tomato paste, water, and jalapeno pepper. Stir and let simmer for 5 minutes.
- Add beans, parsley, oregano, and can of diced tomatoes. Bring to a boil, then reduce heat and let simmer for 20-25 minutes. Enjoy!
- Try pairing chili with avocado, Greek yogurt, tortilla chips.

Dinner

Side Dishes

Pesto Salmon

- 4 Servings
- Prep Time: 5 minutes
- Cook Time: 25 minutes
- Total Time: 30 minutes

Ingredients

- 1 lb or 450 grams of salmon
- 2 tbsp pesto
- 1 tbsp extra virgin olive oil
- 3 cloves garlic
- 1 can (19 oz/540 mL), no salt added white kidney beans
- 2 cups baby spinach

Instructions

- Preheat oven to 425°F and prepare baking sheet with parchment paper.
- Place salmon on the prepared sheet.
- Spread pesto over salmon.
- Bake salmon for 15-17 minutes.
- In a frying pan, heat olive oil and chopped garlic on stove top for 3-5 minutes.
- Add kidney beans, cook for 5 minutes.
- Add baby spinach, cook for a final 3-5 minutes.
- Once salmon is opaque and flakes easily, remove from the oven and top with white beans and spinach mixture.

Simple Edamame Pasta Sauce

4 Servings

Prep Time: 15 minutes

Cook Time: 10 minutes

Total Time: 25 minutes

Ingredients

- 1 cup edamame (shelled, cooked, or thawed if frozen)
- 1 bunch basil
- 2 cups spinach
- 3 cloves garlic
- ¼ cup walnuts
- ½ lemon juiced
- ¼ cup soy milk (unsweetened)
- ¼ cup extra virgin olive oil
- ¼ tsp black pepper
- 8 oz whole grain pasta noodle of choice

Instructions

- Prepare edamame pesto by adding edamame, basil, spinach, garlic, walnuts, lemon juice, soy milk, olive oil, and pepper in a blender or food processor until smooth.
- Boil pasta for 8-10 minutes
- Drain pasta, reserving some pasta water (to thin the sauce).
- In the pot, add cooked noodles and pour pesto over them; use reserved pasta water if needed to thin the sauce.
- Toss pasta with pesto until combined and enjoy!

One Pot Tofu Bolognese

- 4 Servings
- Prep Time: 15 minutes
- Cook Time: 15 minutes
- Total Time: 30 minutes

Ingredients

- 1 cup extra firm tofu (crumbled)
- 1 tbsp extra virgin olive oil
- 1 clove garlic (minced)
- 1 large carrot (diced)
- 1 stalk celery (diced)
- 1 tsp chilli powder
- 1 tsp basil
- ½ tsp oregano
- 2 cups canned low sodium tomato sauce
- 1 cup soy milk (unsweetened)
- 1 tbsp nutritional yeast (optional)

Instructions

- Drain and press tofu for at least 30 minutes.
- In a saucepan, heat olive oil and garlic until browned (2-3 minutes).
- Saute diced carrots and celery for 5 minutes in the saucepan.
- Add crumbled tofu, chili, basil, and oregano; stir to combine.
- Add low-sodium tomato sauce and soy milk; stir.
- Simmer for 10 minutes until heated through, stirring occasionally.
- Serve over pasta of choice.
- Top with nutritional yeast (optional) and enjoy!

Scrambled Tofu

3 Servings

Prep Time: 5 minutes

Cook Time: 10 minutes

Total Time: 15 minutes

Ingredients

- 1 block of firm tofu (approx. 400g)
- 1 tbsp extra virgin olive oil
- 1 onion (diced)
- 1 tomato (diced)
- ½ tbsp turmeric powder
- ½ tbsp nutritional yeast
- Pepper, to taste

Instructions

- Pat tofu with a cloth or paper towels to remove excess water.
- In a pan, heat oil and sauté diced onion and tomato until soft.
- Add tofu by gently crumbling the block with your hands.
- Add turmeric, nutritional yeast, and pepper into the tofu mixture. Mix well.
- Heat until tofu turns golden brown.
- Serve with bread of choice.

Spaghetti Sauce with Lentils

- 7 Servings
- Prep Time: 5 minutes
- Cook Time: 45 minutes
- Total Time: 50 minutes

Ingredients

- 1 cup dry green lentils
- 1 tbsp extra virgin olive oil
- 1 medium onion (diced)
- 4 cloves garlic (minced)
- 1 can (28 oz/ 830 mL)) no salt added crushed tomatoes
- 1 tbsp wine (red or white)
- ½ tbsp thyme (dried)
- ½ tbsp basil (dried)
- ½ tbsp oregano (dried)
- Red pepper flakes (optional)
- Black pepper

Instructions

- Rinse lentils and cook until tender according to the instructions on the package.
- Drain cooked lentils, and set aside.
- In a pot, heat olive oil on medium-high heat. Sauté onion and garlic until aromatic (2-3 min). Then, add the canned crushed tomatoes and cooked lentils.
- Add wine, thyme, basil, and oregano. For a little optional spiciness, add red pepper flakes. Sprinkle black pepper.
- Adjust seasonings to taste.
- Serve with pasta of your choice! Any leftover sauce may be kept frozen.

Peanut Butter Pasta

- 2 Servings
- Prep Time: 10 minutes
- Cook Time: 20 minutes
- Total Time: 30 minutes

Ingredients

- 2 tbsp extra virgin olive oil
- 1 block of extra-firm tofu (~400g), cubed
- 3 cloves garlic (minced finely or grated)
- 1 cup linguine pasta
- 2 tbsp crunchy peanut butter
- 1.5 tsp low sodium soy sauce
- 1 tbsp honey
- 1 tbsp rice vinegar
- ½ cucumber, julienne
- Sesame seeds
- Chili flakes (optional)

Instructions

- Pat tofu dry with a paper towel.
- Heat 1 tbsp. of olive oil on medium-high heat to stir fry tofu until slightly brown, and set aside.
- Then add the other tbsp of olive oil and stir fry garlic until aromatic. Boil the pasta in another pot.
- Take the pan off the heat. Add peanut butter, soy sauce, honey, and rice vinegar. Use hot pasta water to help dissolve peanut butter mixture and adjust consistency. Mix well.
- Drain cooked pasta. Then, toss the pasta in the sauce mixture, adding sliced cucumbers and stir-fried tofu.
- Top with sesame seeds add chili flakes.

Hummus Pizza

1 Serving

Prep Time: 10 minutes

Cook Time: 0 minutes

Total Time: 10 minutes

Ingredients

- 1 whole wheat pita
- 1/4 cup hummus
- 3 tbsp hemp seeds
- 1/4 cup red bell pepper, thinly sliced
- 1/4 cup arugula
- 1/4 cup canned lentils (drained and rinsed)

Instructions

- Spread hummus over the pita and top with hemp seeds.
- Add the bell pepper, arugula and canned lentils.
- Slice and enjoy!

Heart Healthy Pizza

4 Servings

Prep Time: 10 minutes

Cook Time: 20 minutes

Total Time: 30 minutes

Ingredients

- 1 whole wheat pizza dough
- 1 bell pepper, color of choice
- 1 cup white mushrooms sliced
- 1 cup spinach
- 1/2 cup low sodium tomato paste
- 3/4 cup ricotta or shredded low fat mozzarella cheese
- 1 cup of canned lentils (drained and rinsed)
- 1/2 cup fresh basil

Instructions

- Preheat the oven to 400°F.
- Place the dough onto a sheet of parchment paper, and roll it out to about a 1/2 inch thickness.
- Wash and cut bell pepper and mushroom into slices.
- Spread the tomato paste on the dough, then top with peppers, mushroom and spinach.
- Add the ricotta in small dollops and sprinkle the lentils around the pizza.
- Bake the pizza in the oven for 20 minutes.
- Top with some fresh basil.
- Slice and enjoy!

Warm Sweet Potato Lentil Salad

- 4 Servings
- Prep Time: 15 minutes
- Cook Time: 45 minutes
- Total Time: 60 minutes

Ingredients For Salad

- 1 cup dry lentils, picked over and rinsed
- 3 cups water or low sodium
- 2 cups diced sweet potato, approximately 1/2 inch pieces
- 2 tsp extra virgin olive oil
- 1/4 cup chopped parsley
- 2 tablespoon chopped cilantro

Instructions

- Add the lentils to a saucepan along with the water and stir everything together. Bring the lentils to a boil and then reduce to medium-low and cover with a lid. Simmer until the lentils are soft, about 30-35 minutes.
- While the lentils cook line a sheet pan with foil and drizzle the sweet potato chunks with olive. Roast the sweet potato at 425° F for about 20-30 minutes.
- Once the lentils are cooked drain off any excess water and pour into a serving bowl.

Warm Sweet Potato Lentil Salad

Ingredients For Salad Dressing

- 1 tbsp extra virgin olive oil
- 2 tbsp balsamic vinegar
- 1 tbsp Dijon mustard
- 1 tbsp maple syrup
- 1/2 tsp ground cumin
- 1/4 tsp ground coriander

Instructions Continued

- Whisk together all of the ingredients for the salad dressing and pour it over the lentils.
- Add the roasted sweet potato, parsley and cilantro to the bowl and stir everything together until it's well coated.

Hummus Pasta

4 Servings

Prep Time: 5 minutes

Cook Time: 15 minutes

Total Time: 20 minutes

Ingredients

- 8 oz chickpea pasta
- 3/4 cup shelled edamame (frozen)
- 1/2 cup pasta water (reserved after cooking)
- 1 tsp extra virgin olive oil
- 3/4 cup cherry tomato (halved)
- 2/3 cup hummus
- sprinkle of red pepper flakes and fresh basil (optional)

Instructions

- Bring a pot of water to a boil and cook the chickpea pasta according to the package directions.
- During the last two minutes, add the frozen edamame.
- Before draining pasta, set aside 1/2 cup of pasta water to use for your sauce.
- Drain pasta and rinse noodles with water.
- In the same pot over medium heat, add oil and tomatoes and heat through.
- Add the pasta and edamame into the pot and stir in the hummus.
- Add the pasta water one tablespoon at a time and stir until desired consistency of sauce is achieved.
- Top with red pepper flakes and basil.

Curried Potato and Pea Stew

2 Servings

Prep Time: 5 minutes

Cook Time: 50 minutes

Total Time: 55 minutes

Ingredients

- 6 cups of low sodium vegetable broth
- 1 small white onion (diced)
- 2 cloves of garlic (minced)
- 1 cup dried yellow split peas
- 2 cups of mini potatoes (quartered)
- 1 tsp curry powder
- 1.5 cups of frozen shelled edamame

Instructions

- Add a splash of the vegetable broth to a large pot over medium heat. Add the onion, stir, and cook for a couple of minutes. Then add the garlic and cook for another 2-3 minutes, until brown.
- Add the dried split peas and remaining broth. Bring to a rolling boil for 10 minutes, then reduce the heat to low, cover with a lid, and simmer for 15 minutes.
- Add the potatoes and curry powder. Continue to simmer for another 20 minutes, or until it has thickened and most of the liquid has reduced.
- During the last two minutes, add the edamame.

Mediterranean Barley (Side Dish)

4 Servings

Prep Time: 5 minutes

Cook Time: 30 minutes

Total Time: 35 minutes

Ingredients

- 1 cup barley
- 2 cup water
- 1/4 cup pitted kalamata olives
- 1 cup cherry tomatoes (halved)
- 1/4 cup parsley (chopped)
- 1 1/2 tbsp lemon juice

Instructions

- Combine the barley and water together in a saucepan. Place over high heat and bring to a boil.
- Once boiling, reduce heat to a simmer and cover with a lid. Let simmer for 30 minutes or until water is absorbed. Remove lid and fluff with a fork.
- Add the olives, cherry tomatoes and parsley to the barley. Stir to combine. Drizzle with lemon juice and divide evenly between plates. Enjoy!

White Bean Salad (Side Dish)

4 Servings

Prep Time: 10 minutes

Cook Time: 0 minutes

Total Time: 10 minutes

Ingredients

- 1 can (19 oz/540 mL), no salt added white navy beans (drained and rinsed)
- 1 tomato (diced)
- 1/2 red bell pepper (diced)
- 1/4 cup red onion (finely chopped)
- 1/4 cup parsley (finely chopped)
- 2 tbsp extra virgin olive oil
- 2 tbsp balsamic vinegar
- 1 cup baby spinach

Instructions

- Combine the beans, tomato, bell pepper, red onion, parsley in a mixing bowl.
- Add the olive oil and balsamic vinegar. Mix well.
- Split spinach in between bowls and top with bean mixture. Season with additional balsamic vinegar or black pepper if needed. Enjoy!

Beet and Broccoli Salad (Side Dish)

- 4 Servings
- Prep Time: 15 minutes
- Cook Time: 45 minutes
- Total Time: 60 minutes

Ingredients

- 2 beets
- 2 cups broccoli florets lightly steamed
- 1/2 cup prunes, chopped
- 1/4 cup red onion, finely chopped
- 1/4 cup feta cheese diced, optional
- 1/2 cup walnuts, chopped
- 2 tbsp extra virgin olive oil
- 1 tbsp apple cider vinegar
- 1 tsp Dijon mustard

Instructions

- Prepare the Beets: Wash the beets and trim off the tops and roots. Wrap each beet loosely in aluminium foil. Place them on a baking sheet and bake in a preheated oven at 375°F (190°C) for about 45-60 minutes, or until they are easily pierced with a fork. Once done, let them cool until they can be handled, then peel and dice them.
- Prepare the Broccoli: Lightly steam the broccoli florets for about 3-5 minutes until they are bright green and tender-crisp. Let them cool.

Beet and Broccoli Salad (Side Dish)

Instructions Continued

- In a large bowl, combine the diced beets, steamed broccoli, chopped prunes, red onion, feta cheese, and walnuts.
- In a small bowl, whisk together olive oil, apple cider vinegar, Dijon mustard to create the dressing.
- Pour the dressing over the salad and toss gently to combine.
- Serve chilled or at room temperature.

Snacks

Banana Muffins With Lentils

12 Servings

Prep Time: 10 minutes

Cook Time: 22 minutes

Total Time: 32 minutes

Ingredients

- ¼ cup dried red lentils
- ¼ cup old fashioned oats
- 1¼ cup all purpose flour
- ⅓ cup brown sugar
- ¼ tsp baking soda
- 1 tsp baking powder
- ¼ tsp salt
- 1 tbsp cinnamon
- 1 tsp nutmeg
- ½ cup mashed banana
- ½ soy milk (unsweetened)
- 1 egg
- ⅓ cup avocado oil
- ½ cup raisins
- ¼ cup walnuts

Instructions

- Preheat oven to 400˚F and prepare muffin tins with liners.
- Cook lentils and oats in water; simmer for 10 minutes, then let cool.
- Mix dry ingredients: flour, sugar, baking soda, baking powder, salt, cinnamon, and nutmeg.
- Mix wet ingredients: mashed banana, milk, egg, oil, and cooked lentil/oat mixture.
- Add wet ingredients to dry ingredients; mix well.
- Fold in raisins and walnuts.
- Fill muffin tins and bake for 20 minutes or until golden brown.

Edamame Hummus

8 Servings

Prep Time: 5 minutes

Cook Time: 5 minutes

Total Time: 10 minutes

Ingredients

- 2 cups edamame
- ½ cup store bought or premade hummus
- 3 tbsp lemon juice

Instructions

- Combine all ingredients into a food processor or high speed blender and blitz into a smooth paste.
- If you aren't satisfied with the consistency, blend in cold water or extra virgin olive oil, one tablespoon at a time until you are satisfied with the texture and creaminess.

Roasted Black Beans

- 6 Servings
- Prep Time: 1 hour
- Cook Time: 1 hour
- Total Time: 2 hours

Ingredients

- 1 can (19 oz/540 mL) no salt added black beans (drained and rinsed)
- 1 tsp ginger
- 1 tsp turmeric
- 1 tsp cumin
- 1 tsp black pepper
- ⅛ tsp cinnamon
- ⅛ tsp salt
- 1 tbsp extra virgin olive oil

Instructions

- Rinse and let beans dry on a tea towel for at least 1 hour.
- Mix spices in a bowl.
- Add olive oil to spice mixture.
- Coat black beans in spice and olive oil mixture.
- Spread coated beans on a parchment-lined baking sheet in a single layer.
- Bake for 45 to 60 minutes until crispy.
- Watch closely in the final minutes; taste test and remove when beans are browned but not very dark and hard.
- Allow to cool for about 10 minutes.
- Store in an airtight container in a dry cupboard for up to 1 week.

Chocolate Covered Chickpeas

4 Servings

Prep Time: 15 minutes

Cook Time: 15 minutes

Total Time: 30 minutes

Ingredients

- 1 cup canned chickpeas
- ½ cup chocolate chips
- 1 tbsp avocado oil

Instructions

- Preheat the oven to 425°F.
- Open and drain chickpeas, rinse, and pat dry on a kitchen towel.
- Remove loose skins and spread chickpeas on a parchment-covered baking sheet.
- Bake for 20-30 minutes until crispy. Remove loose skins if needed.
- Let chickpeas cool before dipping in chocolate.

Chocolate Covered Chickpeas

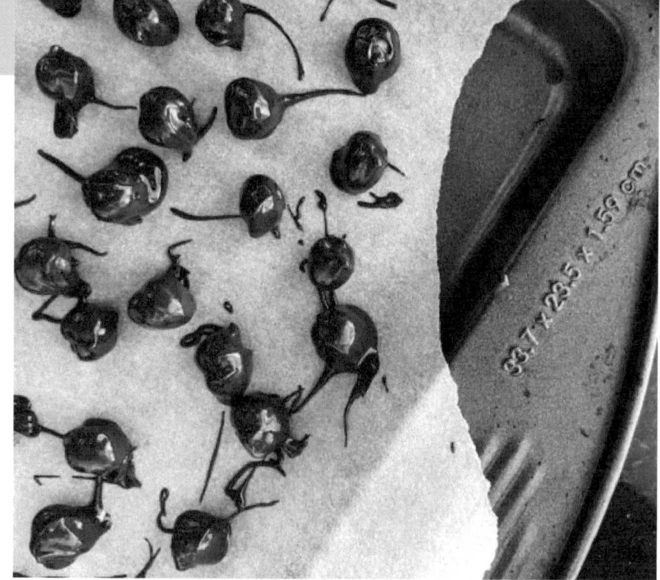

Instructions Continued

- Line another baking sheet with parchment paper.
- Microwave chocolate chips, stirring at 15-second intervals.
- When almost melted, remove and stir to finish melting.
- Add avocado oil to melted chocolate and mix well.
- Combine chickpeas with melted chocolate, stirring to coat evenly.
- Using a fork, transfer coated chickpeas to parchment paper, keeping them separate.
- Remove excess chocolate.
- Transfer to the freezer for 15 minutes to harden.
- Once hardened, individually remove from parchment paper and consume.
- Store in the fridge for up to 5 days.

Turmeric Energy Balls

- 12 Servings
- Prep Time: 20 minutes
- Cook Time: 0 minutes
- Total Time: 20 minutes

Ingredients

- ½ cup old fashioned oats
- 2 tbsp hemp seed
- 2 scoops protein powder
- 1 tsp cinnamon
- 1 tsp turmeric
- ½ tsp ginger
- ⅛ tsp black pepper
- ⅓ cup cashew butter
- ¼ cup honey

Instructions

- Blitz oats in the blender to a flour-like consistency.
- Add hemp seeds, protein powder, cinnamon, turmeric, ginger, and black pepper. Blitz again until mixed.
- In a separate bowl, mix wet ingredients: honey and cashew butter until well combined.
- Combine dry ingredients with wet ingredients, stirring well. Adjust consistency with more oats or nut butter.
- Chill in the refrigerator for 20 minutes.
- Roll the mixture into 1-inch balls.

Sardine Dip with Avocado

4 Servings

Prep Time: 5 minutes

Cook Time: 0 minutes

Total Time: 5 minutes

Ingredients

- 1 tbsp extra virgin olive oil
- 1 tsp black pepper
- 1 medium avocado
- 1 lemon (juiced)
- 1 can (106 g) of low sodium sardines in water
- ¼ cup curly parsley
- 1 clove garlic (minced)
- ¼ cup sweet onion (minced)

Instructions

- In a food blender (or food processor), add the olive oil, black pepper, avocado, lemon juice, and sardines. Process until smooth.
- Take out the mixture and add to a bowl. Add parsley, garlic and onions. Season according to taste.
- Enjoy!

No Bake Pumpkin Protein Balls

12 Servings

Prep Time: 10 minutes

Cook Time: 0 minutes

Total Time: 10 minutes

Ingredients

- 1 cup old fashioned oats
- 3 tbsp flaxseed (ground)
- 1 tsp cinnamon
- ½ tsp ginger
- ½ tsp nutmeg
- ⅛ tsp salt
- ½ cup almond butter
- ¼ cup pumpkin puree
- 3 tbsp honey
- 2 tbsp chocolate chips

Instructions

- In a large bowl, add the oats, flaxseed, cinnamon, ginger, nutmeg, and salt. Use a wooden spoon to mix well.
- Add the almond butter, pumpkin puree, and honey. Mix until all the ingredients are combined.
- Add in the chocolate chips. Roll the mixture into small balls. Serve immediately or store in a refrigerator for up to 5 days. Enjoy!

Guacamole Madness

8 Servings

Prep Time: 10 minutes

Cook Time: 0 minutes

Total Time: 10 minutes

Ingredients

- 4 ripe avocados
- 1 medium tomato (diced)
- 2 cloves garlic (minced)
- ⅓ red onion (diced)
- 1 tsp salt
- 1 tsp pepper
- 1 tbsp extra virgin olive oil
- ⅓ cup parsley (optional)
- 2 limes (juiced)

Instructions

- Prepare all ingredients and set aside in a small bowl.
- In a bowl, using a fork mash the avocados until everything is completely smooth and consistent.
- Then add the tomatoes, garlic, onions, salt, pepper, olive oil, and parsley into the bowl containing mashes avocados.
- Add the freshly squeezed lime juice into the bowl with the ingredients and mix with a spoon.
- Serve a portion with some pita chips, celery, or carrots. Enjoy!

Quick Chickpea Salad

3 Servings

Prep Time: 5 minutes

Cook Time: 15 hour

Total Time: 20 minutes

Ingredients

- 1 can (19 oz/540 mL) no salt added chickpeas (drained & rinsed)
- ¼ cup parsley (minced)
- 1 small sweet onion (diced)
- ½ cup tomato (diced)
- ½ cup cucumbers (diced)
- 2 cloves garlic (minced)
- ½ cup feta cheese (crumbled)
- 1 lemon (squeezed)
- 1 tbsp pesto
- 1 tbsp extra virgin olive oil
- 1 tsp ground pepper

Instructions

- Transfer chickpeas to a bowl where the rest of ingredients will be mixed.
- Add parsley, onions, tomatoes, cucumber, garlic and feta into a bowl with the chickpeas. Add the lemon juice, pesto, oil, pepper and mix. Add olive oil for taste and mix thoroughly
- Serve a portion and enjoy! Refrigerate the rest for up to 5 days.

No Bake Oat Granola Bars

- 12 Servings
- Prep Time: 10 minutes
- Cook Time: 60 minutes
- Total Time: 70 minutes

Ingredients

Dry Ingredients

- 1 cup old-fashioned oats
- ¼ cup sunflower seeds
- ¼ cup almonds
- 1 tsp cinnamon (ground)
- 1 tsp nutmeg (ground)
- ¼ cup cranberries (dried)

Wet Ingredients

- ⅓ cup extra virgin olive oil
- ½ cup honey
- 2 tbsp almond butter
- 1 tsp vanilla extract

Other

- 4 medjool dates (pitted)

Instructions

- In a large bowl, add all the dry ingredients and set aside.
- In a small saucepan, add all wet ingredients. Start with the olive oil first to prevent any burning and sticking. And whisk until the mixture is well combined. Stir for around 1-3 minutes at low-medium heat to prevent burning.

No Bake Oat Granola Bars

Instructions Continued

- In a food processor, add the pitted dates and process until the dates are a sticky paste and have a smooth consistency. Add the warm wet ingredients into the food processor and process until a smooth consistency is reached.
- Then, pour the food processor mixture into the dry ingredients. Using a spatula, stir until fully mixed.
- Place parchment paper in a baking pan, and pour the mixture into the pan. Spread the mixture flat and make sure to to press down flat to ensure that the bars will hold together.
- Put the baking pan into the fridge and leave to cool for 60 minutes.
- After chilling, take out the pan and cut the granola into small bars. Store the remaining granola bars in an airtight container and enjoy!

No Bake Cranberry Orange Granola Bars

- 8 Servings
- Prep Time: 15 minutes
- Cook Time: 8 hours
- Total Time: 8 hours 15 minutes

Ingredients

- 1 ½ cup rolled oats
- ½ cup roasted nuts of choice
- 1 ½ cup cranberries (dried)
- ¼ tsp salt
- 1 tsp orange zest
- 2 tbsp orange juice
- ¼ cup honey
- ¼ cup almond butter
- ¼ cup avocado oil
- 1 tsp vanilla extract

Instructions

- Line a baking pan (I used a 9" x 3" baking pan) with parchment paper
- Toast oats on low-medium heat for about 5 minutes
- Place nuts and cranberries in a food processor, and give it a quick run so they are broken up but not powdered (about 5-8 seconds).

No Bake Cranberry Orange Granola Bars

Instructions Continued

- In a bowl, combine the nuts and cranberries with oats, salt, and orange zest. Mix well.
- In another bowl, add orange juice, honey, almond butter, avocado oil, and vanilla extract. Mix well.
- Pour the liquid ingredients into the dry ingredients and mix until the ingredients are well incorporated. Tip: This is the time when slight adjustments may be required. Mixing takes some effort because the mixture is thick and there should be no dry oats remaining. if you feel the mixture is too thin and really easy to mix, I suggest adding more oats to the mixture; on the other hand, if you see a lot of oats still dry and not incorporated add slightly more liquid of the liquid ingredients.
- Pour the mixture into the baking pan prepared in step 1. Use a rubber spatula to level off the mixture so it is evenly spread across the baking sheet with no lumps.
- Cover the baking pan with plastic wrap and let it sit in the refrigerator for about 8 hours.
- Remove the granola mixture from the pan and cut into 8 pieces. Enjoy!

Prune Banana Bread

10 Servings

Prep Time: 15 minutes

Cook Time: 50 minutes

Total Time: 1 hours 5 minutes

Ingredients

- 2 ripe bananas
- 1 cup prunes pitted, chopped
- 1/3 cup unsweetened applesauce
- 1/2 cup maple syrup
- 2 eggs
- 1 tsp vanilla extract
- 1 3/4 cup whole wheat flour
- 1 tsp baking soda
- 1/2 tsp salt
- 1 tsp cinnamon
- 1/2 cup walnuts

Instructions

- Preheat your oven to 350°F (175°C). Grease a 9×5 inch loaf pan or line it with parchment paper.
- In a large bowl, mash the bananas with a fork until smooth. Stir in the chopped prunes and applesauce.
- Beat in the maple syrup, eggs, and vanilla extract until well combined.

Prune Banana Bread

Instructions Continued

- In another bowl, whisk together the whole wheat flour, baking soda, salt, and cinnamon.
- Gradually add the dry ingredients to the wet ingredients, stirring until just combined. Avoid overmixing. If using, fold in the chopped nuts.
- Pour the batter into the prepared loaf pan and smooth the top.
- Bake for 50 minutes, or until a toothpick inserted into the center of the bread comes out clean.
- Allow the prune banana bread to cool in the pan for about 10 minutes, then transfer it to a wire rack to cool completely.

Favorite Recipes

Now it's your turn!

Do you have favorite cholesterol lowering recipes to add to this cookbook?

I've included a few blank pages to add recipes that your family loves!

___ Servings

Prep Time: ___ minutes

Cook Time: ___ minutes

Total Time: __ minutes

Ingredients

- ______________________
- ______________________
- ______________________
- ______________________
- ______________________
- ______________________
- ______________________
- ______________________
- ______________________

Instructions

____

____

____

____

____

____

____

____

____

____

____

____

___ Servings

Prep Time: ___ minutes

Cook Time: ___ minutes

Total Time: __ minutes

Ingredients

- ______________________________
- ______________________________
- ______________________________
- ______________________________
- ______________________________
- ______________________________
- ______________________________
- ______________________________
- ______________________________

Instructions

____

____

____

____

____

____

____

____

____

____

____

____

___ Servings

Prep Time: ___ minutes

Cook Time: ___ minutes

Total Time: __ minutes

Ingredients

- ______________________________
- ______________________________
- ______________________________
- ______________________________
- ______________________________
- ______________________________
- ______________________________
- ______________________________
- ______________________________

Instructions

____

____

____

____

____

____

____

____

____

____

____

____

___ Servings

Prep Time: ___ minutes

Cook Time: ___ minutes

Total Time: __ minutes

Ingredients

- ______________________________
- ______________________________
- ______________________________
- ______________________________
- ______________________________
- ______________________________
- ______________________________
- ______________________________
- ______________________________

Instructions

____

____

____

____

____

____

____

____

____

____

____

____

___ Servings

Prep Time: ___ minutes

Cook Time: ___ minutes

Total Time: __ minutes

Ingredients

- ______________________________
- ______________________________
- ______________________________
- ______________________________
- ______________________________
- ______________________________
- ______________________________
- ______________________________
- ______________________________

Instructions

____

____

____

____

____

____

____

____

____

____

____

____

___ Servings

Prep Time: ___ minutes

Cook Time: ___ minutes

Total Time: __ minutes

Ingredients

- ____________________
- ____________________
- ____________________
- ____________________
- ____________________
- ____________________
- ____________________
- ____________________
- ____________________

Instructions

____

____

____

____

____

____

____

____

____

____

____

____

Trackers

I've added two helpful tools to assist you in maintaining your health and diet goals:

The Cholesterol Monitoring Tool

This is an excellent resource for logging and keeping up with your routine lab appointments. This tool is not just about tracking your cholesterol levels; it's about setting personalized targets tailored to your health needs. It allows you to monitor changes in your cholesterol over time and understand patterns.

The Daily Portfolio Checklist

This checklist will aid you in staying committed and keeping your diet on course every day. Checking off each item on the checklist will empower you to make healthier choices that align with the Portfolio Diet. The tool encourages daily adherence to help establish healthy eating habits.

Cholesterol Monitoring

Date	Total Cholesterol	LDL	HDL	Triglycerides	Notes

Cholesterol Monitoring

Date	Total Cholesterol	LDL	HDL	Triglycerides	Notes

The Portfolio Diet Checklist

Food Groups	Intake (g/day)	Serving per day	Mon	Tue	Wed	Thu	Fri	Sat	Sun
Nuts (whole, nut butters)	50g	1	☐	☐	☐	☐	☐	☐	☐
Soluble Fiber (okra, psyllium pears, avocado, barley)	10-25g	4-5	☐ ☐ ☐ ☐	☐ ☐ ☐ ☐	☐ ☐ ☐ ☐	☐ ☐ ☐ ☐	☐ ☐ ☐ ☐	☐ ☐ ☐ ☐	☐ ☐ ☐ ☐
Plant Protein (legumes pulses, soy beverage tofu)	50g	3	☐ ☐ ☐	☐ ☐ ☐	☐ ☐ ☐	☐ ☐ ☐	☐ ☐ ☐	☐ ☐ ☐	☐ ☐ ☐
Plant Sterols (fortified foods or supplem -ents)	2g	1-2	☐ ☐	☐ ☐	☐ ☐	☐ ☐	☐ ☐	☐ ☐	☐ ☐

The Portfolio Diet Checklist

Food Groups	Intake (g/day)	Serving per day	Mon	Tue	Wed	Thu	Fri	Sat	Sun
Nuts (whole, nut butters)	50g	1	☐	☐	☐	☐	☐	☐	☐
Soluble Fiber (okra, psyllium pears, avocado, barley)	10-25g	4-5	☐ ☐ ☐ ☐	☐ ☐ ☐ ☐	☐ ☐ ☐ ☐	☐ ☐ ☐ ☐	☐ ☐ ☐ ☐	☐ ☐ ☐ ☐	☐ ☐ ☐ ☐
Plant Protein (legumes pulses, soy beverage tofu)	50g	3	☐ ☐ ☐	☐ ☐ ☐	☐ ☐ ☐	☐ ☐ ☐	☐ ☐ ☐	☐ ☐ ☐	☐ ☐ ☐
Plant Sterols (fortified foods or supplem -ents)	2g	1-2	☐ ☐	☐ ☐	☐ ☐	☐ ☐	☐ ☐	☐ ☐	☐ ☐

The Portfolio Diet Checklist

Food Groups	Intake (g/day)	Serving per day	Mon	Tue	Wed	Thu	Fri	Sat	Sun
Nuts (whole, nut butters)	50g	1	☐	☐	☐	☐	☐	☐	☐
Soluble Fiber (okra, psyllium pears, avocado, barley)	10-25g	4-5	☐ ☐ ☐ ☐	☐ ☐ ☐ ☐	☐ ☐ ☐ ☐	☐ ☐ ☐ ☐	☐ ☐ ☐ ☐	☐ ☐ ☐ ☐	☐ ☐ ☐ ☐
Plant Protein (legumes pulses, soy beverage tofu)	50g	3	☐ ☐ ☐	☐ ☐ ☐	☐ ☐ ☐	☐ ☐ ☐	☐ ☐ ☐	☐ ☐ ☐	☐ ☐ ☐
Plant Sterols (fortified foods or supplem -ents)	2g	1-2	☐ ☐	☐ ☐	☐ ☐	☐ ☐	☐ ☐	☐ ☐	☐ ☐

The Portfolio Diet Checklist

Food Groups	Intake (g/day)	Serving per day	Mon	Tue	Wed	Thu	Fri	Sat	Sun
Nuts (whole, nut butters)	50g	1	☐	☐	☐	☐	☐	☐	☐
Soluble Fiber (okra, psyllium pears, avocado, barley)	10-25g	4-5	☐ ☐ ☐ ☐	☐ ☐ ☐ ☐	☐ ☐ ☐ ☐	☐ ☐ ☐ ☐	☐ ☐ ☐ ☐	☐ ☐ ☐ ☐	☐ ☐ ☐ ☐
Plant Protein (legumes pulses, soy beverage tofu)	50g	3	☐ ☐ ☐	☐ ☐ ☐	☐ ☐ ☐	☐ ☐ ☐	☐ ☐ ☐	☐ ☐ ☐	☐ ☐ ☐
Plant Sterols (fortified foods or supplem -ents)	2g	1-2	☐ ☐	☐ ☐	☐ ☐	☐ ☐	☐ ☐	☐ ☐	☐ ☐

Bibliography

1. Jenkins, D. J. A., Josse, A. R., Wong, J. M. W., Nguyen, T. H., & Kendall, C. W. C. (2007). The Portfolio Diet for cardiovascular risk reduction. Current Atherosclerosis Reports, 9(6), 501–507.

2. Jenkins, D. J., Kendall, C. W., Faulkner, D. A., Nguyen, T., Kemp, T., Marchie, A., Wong, J. M., de Souza, R., Emam, A., Vidgen, E., Trautwein, E. A., Lapsley, K. G., Holmes, C., Josse, R. G., Leiter, L. A., Connelly, P. W., & Singer, W. (2006). Assessment of the longer-term effects of a dietary portfolio of cholesterol-lowering foods in hypercholesterolemia. The American Journal of Clinical Nutrition, 83(3), 582–591.)

3. Chiavaroli, L., Nishi, S. K., Khan, T. A., Braunstein, C. R., Glenn, A. J., Mejia, S. B., Rahelić, D., Kahleová, H., Salas-Salvadó, J., Jenkins, D. J. A., Kendall, C. W. C., & Sievenpiper, J. L. (2018). Portfolio Dietary Pattern and Cardiovascular Disease: A Systematic Review and Meta-analysis of Controlled Trials. Progress in Cardiovascular Diseases, 61(1), 43–53.

4. Jenkins, D. J. A., Kendall, C. W. C., Lapsley, K. G., Josse, R. G., Leiter, L. A., Singer, W., Connelly, P. W., Marchie, A., Faulkner, D. A., Wong, J. M. W., De Souza, R., Emam, A., Parker, T. L., Vidgen, E., & Trautwein, E. A. (2005). Direct comparison of a dietary portfolio of cholesterol-lowering foods with a statin in hypercholesterolemic participants. The American Journal of Clinical Nutrition, 81(2), 380–387.

5. Holscher, H. D. (2017). Dietary fiber and prebiotics and the gastrointestinal microbiota. Gut Microbes, 8(2), 172–184.

6. Jenkins, D. J. A., Jones, P. J. H., Lamarche, B., Kendall, C. W. C., Faulkner, D., Cermakova, L., Gigleux, I., Ramprasath, V., de Souza, R., Ireland, C., Patel, D., Srichaikul, K., Abdulnour, S., Bashyam, B., Collier, C., Hoshizaki, S., Josse, R. G., Leiter, L. A., Connelly, P. W., & Frohlich, J. (2011). Effect of a Dietary Portfolio of Cholesterol-Lowering Foods Given at 2 Levels of Intensity of Dietary Advice on Serum Lipids in Hyperlipidemia: A Randomized Controlled Trial. JAMA : the Journal of the American Medical Association, 306(8), 831–839.

7. Li, S. S., Blanco Mejia, S., Lytvyn, L., Stewart, S. E., Viguiliouk, E., Ha, V., Souza, R. J., Leiter, L. A., Kendall, C. W. C., Jenkins, D. J. A., & Sievenpiper, J. L. (2017). Effect of Plant Protein on Blood Lipids: A Systematic Review and Meta-Analysis of Randomized Controlled Trials. Journal of the American Heart Association, 6(12), n/a.

8. Nishi, S. K., Viguiliouk, E., Blanco Mejia, S., Kendall, C. W. C., Bazinet, R. P., Hanley, A. J., Comelli, E. M., Salas Salvadó, J., Jenkins, D. J. A., & Sievenpiper, J. L. (2021). Are fatty nuts a weighty concern? A systematic review and meta-analysis and dose–response meta-regression of prospective cohorts and randomized controlled trials. Obesity Reviews, 22(11), e13330-n/a.

9. AbuMweis, S. S., Marinangeli, C. P. F., Frohlich, J., & Jones, P. J. H. (2014). Implementing phytosterols into medical practice as a cholesterol-lowering strategy: overview of efficacy, effectiveness, and safety. Canadian Journal of Cardiology, 30(10), 1225.

10. Alberta Health Services. (2018). Portfolio eating pattern. https://www.albertahealthservices.ca/assets/info/nutrition/if-nfs-portfolio-eating-pattern-form.pdf

11. Hamilton Health Sciences. Portfolio Diet. (2013, May 2). https://www.hamiltonhealthsciences.ca/wp-content/uploads/2019/08/PortfolioDiet-trh.pdf

12. Bouzek, A. (2024, January 12). Soluble Fiber Foods Chart + free PDF. The Geriatric Dietitian. https://thegeriatricdietitian.com/soluble-fiber-foods-chart/#h-soluble-fiber-foods-chart

13. London Health Sciences Centre. (n.d.). The Portfolio Diet - lipid genetics clinic. http://www.lipidgeneticsclinic.ca/pdf/2015%2009%2022%20The%20Portfolio%20Diet.pdf

Oh hey there.

I am so happy to see you.

Hi, I'm Veronica, The Heart Dietitian!

I believe you have control over your heart disease by eating well.

My mission is to translate heart-healthy research into small lifestyle changes that make you feel confident about feeding your heart.

This book is full of Dietitian approved information and recipes to help you make thoughtful (and delicious!) food choices that will set you up for success to live a longer, healthier life.

Remember it's not about doing everything at once but making one small change at a time. You can do it!

Disclaimer:
I am a dietitian, but I'm not your dietitian. This book includes information for the general public and should not be considered medical advice. By purchasing this book, no Registered Dietitian-Client relationship is formed.

I cannot dispense individual dietary recommendations without meeting with you personally and assessing your situation. Always consult a physician or health care professional if you have any medical concerns to get the individualized care you need.

About The Author

Veronica Rouse, MAN, RD, CDE is a Registered Dietitian Nutritionist, writer, speaker, consultant and communication specialist. Her expertise has been quoted in dozens of respected media outlets such as Forbes Health, Medical News Today, Shape and Men's Health.

She is the founder of The Heart Dietitian Food Blog where she provides delicious and straight forward heart healthy recipes as well as science backed information on a variety of heart health topics. Additionally, Veronica is the author of Easy Steps To Lower Cholesterol: The Portfolio Diet which provides a road map for how and what to eat to lower LDL ("bad") cholesterol.

Veronica cares about helping people make smart food choices to improve their heart health and does so by harmonizing heart health research with real-life eating habits. She believes that making small and lasting changes to how we eat can make a big difference for our hearts.

You can connect with Veronica by visiting her blog https://theheartdietitian.com/

Learn More

If you liked this book, please kindly **consider leaving a rating on Amazon**. Your feedback helps more people find it and learn how to lower their cholesterol with food.

@TheHeartDietitian

@TheHeartDietitian

www.theheartdietitian.com

Made in the USA
Columbia, SC
05 September 2024

41804518R00080